D0343552

LITTLE
HEBREW ALPHABET
Coloring Book

Jill Dubin

Dover Publications, Inc.
New York

Published in Canada by General Publishing Company, Ltd., 30 Lesmill Road, Don Mills, Toronto, Ontario.

Published in the United Kingdom by Constable and Company, Ltd., 3 The Lanchesters, 162–164 Fulham Palace Road, London W6 9ER.

Little Hebrew Alphabet Coloring Book is a new work, first published by Dover Publications, Inc., in 1992.

International Standard Book Number: 0-486-27018-1

Manufactured in the United States of America
Dover Publications, Inc., 31 East 2nd Street, Mineola, N.Y. 11501

LITTLE HEBREW ALPHABET

Coloring Book

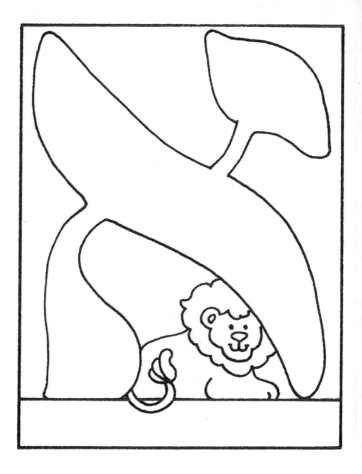

אַרְיֵה

8

בַּיִת

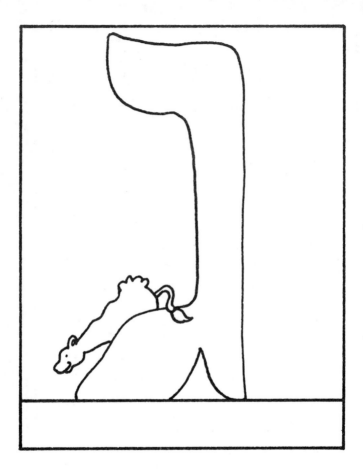

גָּמָל

דָּג

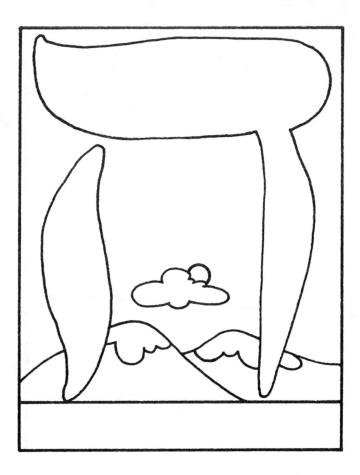

הַר

16

וֶרֶד

זְאֵב

חָתוּל

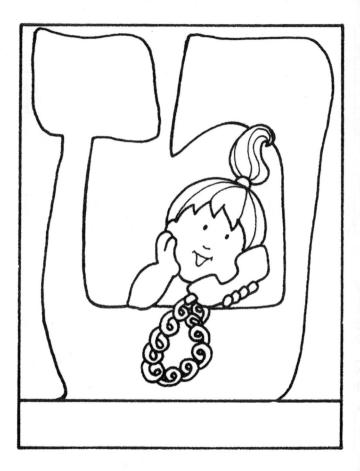

טֶלֶפוֹן

יְלָדִים

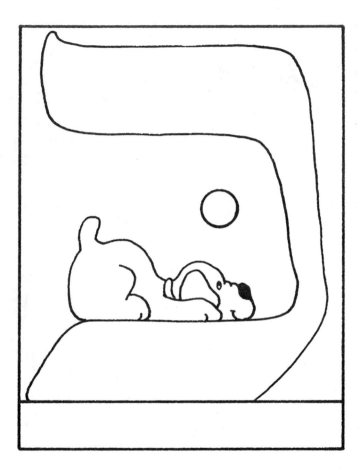

כֶּלֶב

לֵיצָן

מֶלֶךְ

נָמֵר

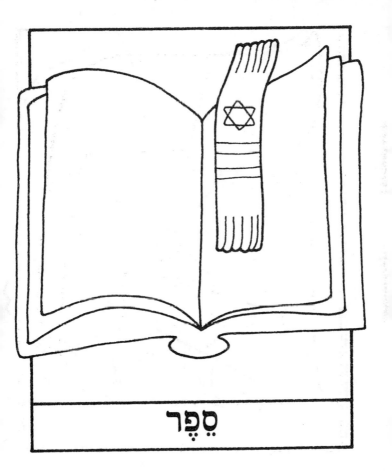

סֵפֶר

עֵץ

38

פָּרָה

39

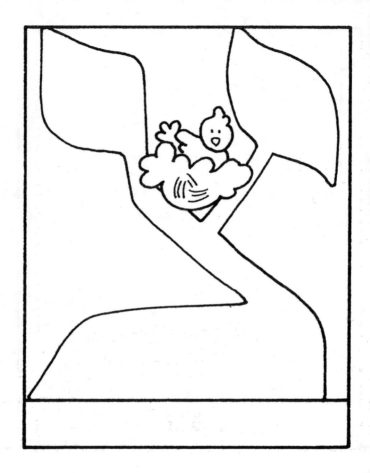

צִיפּוֹר

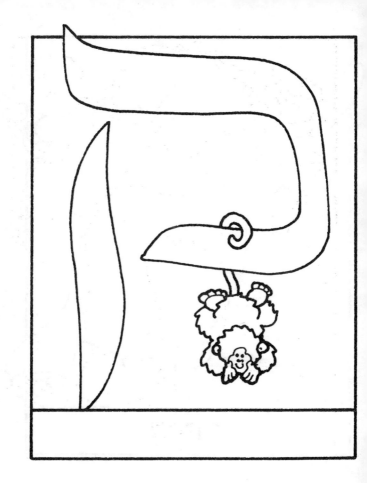

קוֹף

44

רַכֶּבֶת

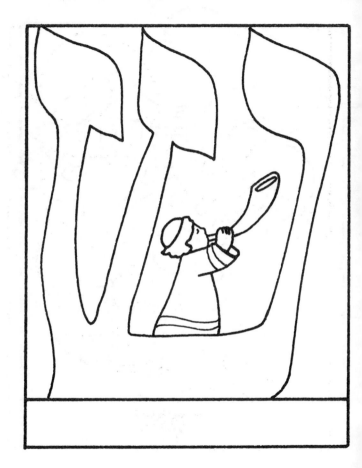

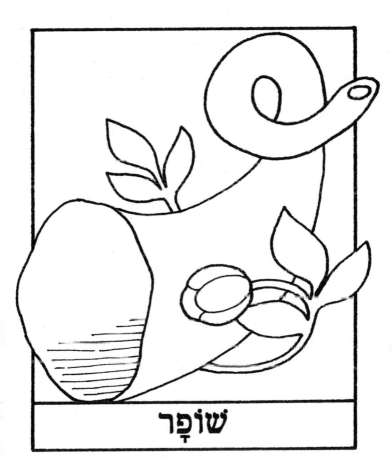

שׁוֹפָר

תַּפּוּחַ

Note

Whether children are studying Hebrew as a first or as a second language, they need to learn the alphabet and acquire useful vocabulary. One of the most enjoyable ways to help them remember both the letters of the alphabet and new words is by activity, especially in the form of coloring.

The present book contains a full Hebrew alphabet keyed to essential everyday words, to names of animals and familiar objects, all charmingly illustrated by Jill Dubin, who has designed many books on Jewish subjects.

To help children "think in Hebrew," only the Hebrew words for the items illustrated appear in the main part of the book. Following this "Note" is a section called "Guide to the Book." In that section the full word list is repeated, not only with English equivalents (forming a handy glossary), but also with a guide to their pronunciation and with a rundown of the Hebrew letters, their names (in English transliteration) and their pronunciation.

It should be remembered that all the Hebrew letters represent consonants (although a few of them often team up with vowels to help represent vowel sounds). In newspapers and everyday books for adults, the vowels are not written. In language reference books, in religious texts and in books for children, like this one, the vowels are indicated by special signs underneath the letters. The vowel system is not really difficult, but is a little too complicated to explain in a book of this length, which is mainly intended to teach the alphabet (the consonants).

No attempt is made in this book to teach any grammar whatsoever. The words in this book are in their "dictionary form"— as they would appear in a mere listing. They can change in different ways when endings or prefixes are added to them. Only further study of grammar will show you how to use them in sentences. We hope this book will encourage you to go on and really learn this beautiful and interesting language.

Guide to the Book

PAGES	HEBREW LETTER	NAME OF LETTER	PRONUNCIATION OF LETTER	WORD ILLUSTRATED	PRONUNCIATION OF WORD	MEANING OF WORD
6 & 7	א	alef	[silent]	אַרְיֵה	ar-YAY	lion
8 & 9	בּ	bet	[with dot:] b, [without dot:] v	בַּיִת	BAH-yeet	house
10 & 11	ג	gimel	g [as in "go"]	גָּמָל	gah-MAHL	camel

PAGES	HEBREW LETTER	NAME OF LETTER	PRONUNCIATION OF LETTER	WORD ILLUSTRATED	PRONUNCIATION OF WORD	MEANING OF WORD
12 & 13	ד	dalet	d	דָג	dahg	fish
14 & 15	ה	hay	h, [silent at end of word]	הַר	har	mountain
16 & 17	ו	vav	v, [וֹ = oh, וּ = oo]	וֶרֶד	VEH-red	rose
18 & 19	ז	zayin	z	זְאֵב	zuh-AYV	wolf
20 & 21	ח	chet (khet)	kh [that is, like "ch" in Scottish "loch," not as in "cheer"]	חָתוּל	kha-TOOL	cat

56

No.	Letter	Name	Sound	Hebrew	Pronunciation	Meaning
22 & 23	ט	tet	t	טֶלֶפוֹן	teh-leh-FOHN	telephone
24 & 25	י	yood	[at beginning of syllable:] y (as in "yes"), [at middle or end of syllable:] ee	יְלָדִים	yuh-lah-DEEM	children
26 & 27 [at end of word:] ך	כ	kaf	[with dot:] k, [without dot:] kh	כֶּלֶב	KEH-lev	dog
28 & 29	ל	lamed	l	לֵצָן	lay-TSAHN	clown

PAGES	HEBREW LETTER	NAME OF LETTER	PRONUNCIATION OF LETTER	WORD ILLUSTRATED	PRONUNCIATION OF WORD	MEANING OF WORD
30 & 31 [at end of word:]	מ ם	mem	m	מֶלֶךְ	MEH-lekh	king
32 & 33 [at end of word:]	נ ן	noon	n	נָמֵר	nah-MAYR	tiger
34 & 35	ס	samech (samekh)	s	סֵפֶר	SAY-fehr	book
36 & 37	ע	ayin	[silent]	עֵץ	ayts	tree

38 & 39	פ	pay	[with dot:] p, [without dot:] f	פָּרָה	pah-RAH	cow
[at end of word:]	ף					
40 & 41	צ	tzadee (tsadee)	ts	צִפּוֹר	tsee-POHR	bird
[at end of word:]	ץ					
42 & 43	ק	kuf	k	קוֹף	kohf	monkey
44 & 45	ר	raysh	r	רַכֶּבֶת	rah-KEH-vet	train

59

PAGES	HEBREW LETTER	NAME OF LETTER	PRONUNCIATION OF LETTER	WORD ILLUSTRATED	PRONUNCIATION OF WORD	MEANING OF WORD
46 & 47	שׁ*	shin*	sh*	שׁוֹפָר	shoh-FAHR	horn, shofar
48 & 49	ת	tav	t [with or without dot]	תַּפּוּחַ	tah-POO-ahkh	apple

*When this letter has its dot at the left side, שׂ , the name of the letter is "sin" and it is pronounced "s," as in the word שֵׂכֶל , pronounced "SAY-khel," meaning "good sense."